Phonics a Word Study

Acknowledgments

Photos: Pages 6, 7, 9, 12, 13, 15, 18 www.photos.com; Page 10 www.en.wikipedia.org; Page 16 www.istockphoto.com/eurobanks; Page 19 www.istockphoto.com/laartist

Continental Press

ISBN 978-0-8454-3850-3

Copyright © 2008 The Continental Press, Inc.

No part of this publication may be reproduced in any form or by any means, electronic, mechanical, photocopying, recording, or otherwise, without the prior written permission of the publisher. All rights reserved. Printed in the United States of America.

Table of Contents

Initial Consonants 3
Final Consonants. 4
Medial Consonants 5
Short Vowel **a**. 6
Long Vowel **a** 7
Review Short and Long Vowel **a** 8
Short Vowel **e**. 9
Long Vowel **e** 10
Review Short and Long Vowel **e** 11
Short Vowel **i** 12
Long Vowel **i** 13
Review Short and Long Vowel **i** 14
Short Vowel **o**. 15
Long Vowel **o** 16
Review Short and Long Vowel **o** 17
Short Vowel **u**. 18
Long Vowel **u** 19
Review Short and Long Vowel **u** 20
Review Short Vowels 21
Review Long Vowels 22
Review Short and Long Vowels. 23
Vowel Spellings **oa, ai,** and **ee**. 24
Two Sounds of the Letters **ea** 25
Sounds of the Spellings **er, ir,** and **ur** 26
Sounds of the Spellings **ar** and **or**. 27
Review Sounds of the Spellings
   ir, er, ur, or, and **ar** 28
Consonant Digraphs **sh** and **th**. 29
Consonant Digraphs **ch** and **tch** 30
Consonant Digraphs **ng** and **ck** 31
Review Consonant Digraphs **sh, ch,**
   th, tch, ck, and **ng**. 32
Sounds of the Consonant **c** /k/ and /s/ . . 33
Sounds of the Consonant **g** /g/ and /j/ . . 34
Review Consonants **c** and **g** 35
Initial Consonant Blends with **r** 36
Initial Consonant Blends with **l** 37
Initial Consonant Blends with **s** 38
Review Initial Consonant Blends 39
Final Consonant Blends with **n**. 40
Final Consonant Blends with **l**. 41
Review Final Consonant Blends 42

The Spellings **wh** and **mb** 43
The Spellings **kn** and **wr** 44
Review the Spellings **kn, wr, wh,** and **mb** . 45
Sounds of the Spelling **oo** 46
Sounds of the Spellings **ou** and **ow**. 47
The Diphthongs **oi** and **oy** 48
Three Sounds of the Spelling **ear** 49
Sound of the Spelling **ew**. 50
Sound of the Letter **a** Before **ll, lk,** and **w** . . 51
Review Vowel Digraphs. 52
Doubling the Final Consonant Before
   Adding **-y, -ing,** and **-ed** 53
Changing **y** to **i** Before Adding **-es** or **-ed** . 54
Changing Root Words Before
   Adding **-y, -ing, -ed,** or **-es** 55
Adding **-s** or **-es** to Form Plurals 56
Dropping **e** Before Adding **-ed,**
   -es, -ing, or **-er** 57
Review Adding Endings. 58
Review Adding Endings. 59
The Ending **-ly** 60
The Ending **-ful** 61
The Prefix **un-** 62
The Prefix **re-** 63
Review **un-, re-, -ly,** and **-ful** 64
Review Prefixes and Endings 65
Compound Words 66
Compound Words 67
Contractions with **not** 68
Contractions with Pronouns 69
Review Compound Words and
   Contractions. 70
Syllables 71
Vowel Sounds and Syllables 72
Dividing Syllables—Double Consonants. . . 73
Dividing Syllables—Unlike Consonants . . . 74
Dividing Syllables—Consonant Before **le** . . 75
Review Syllables 76
Assessment. 77
Assessment. 78
Assessment. 79
Assessment. 80

Circle the letter that stands for the sound you hear at the beginning of the picture name.

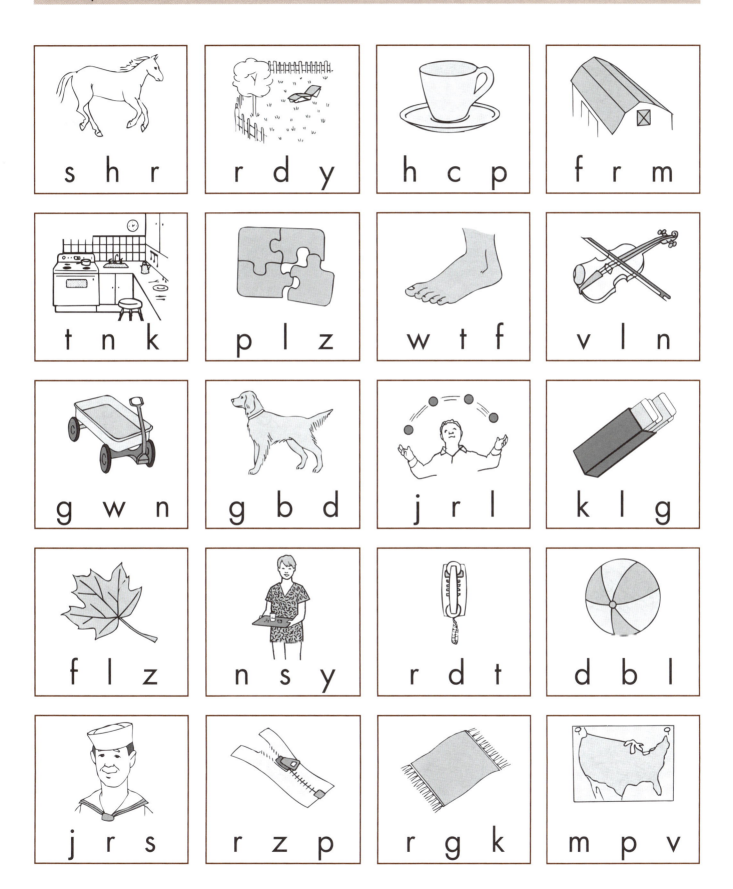

Initial Consonants

Circle the letter that stands for the sound you hear at the end of the picture name.

4 Final Consonants

Write the letter that stands for the consonant sound you hear in the middle of the picture name.

Medial Consonants

Short Vowel

a

Circle the letter **a** under the picture if you hear the short vowel sound in **cat.**

Long Vowel

Say the picture name. Write the letter ā with a line over it if you hear the long vowel sound in **gate**.

Long Vowel **a**   7

Write the vowel sound you hear in the picture name.
Put a line over long vowel ā.

Short Vowel

Circle the letter **e** under the picture if you hear the short vowel sound in **jet**.

Short Vowel **e**

Long Vowel

Say the picture name. Write the letter **ē** with a line over it if you hear the long vowel sound in **jeep**.

Write the vowel sound you hear in the picture name. Put a line over long vowel ē.

Review Short and Long Vowel e

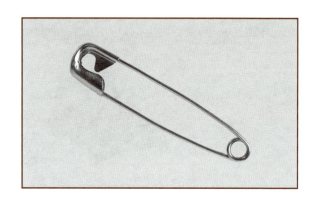

Short Vowel

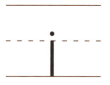

Circle the letter **i** under the picture if you hear the short vowel sound in **pin.**

Long Vowel

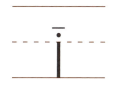

Say the picture name. Write the letter **ī** with a line over it if you hear the long vowel sound in **kite.**

Long Vowel i

Write the vowel sound you hear in the picture name. Put a line over long vowel **ī**.

14 Review Short and Long Vowel i

Short Vowel

o

Circle the letter **o** under the picture if you hear the short vowel sound in **clock.**

Long Vowel

Say the picture name. Write the letter ō with a line over it if you hear the long vowel sound in **hose**.

16 Long Vowel **o**

Write the vowel sound you hear in the picture name. Put a line over long vowel ō.

 ō

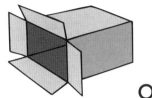 o

Review Short and Long Vowel o

Short Vowel

Circle the letter **u** under the picture if you hear the short vowel sound in **cup**.

18 Short Vowel **u**

Long Vowel

Say the picture name. Write the letter **ū** with a line over it if you hear the long vowel sound in **cubes** or **juice**.

Write the vowel sound you hear in the picture name. Put a line over long vowel **ū.**

 ū  u

20 Review Short and Long Vowel **u**

Trace the letter of each short vowel sound. Write the letter that stands for the short vowel sound you hear in the picture name.

a   e   i   o   u

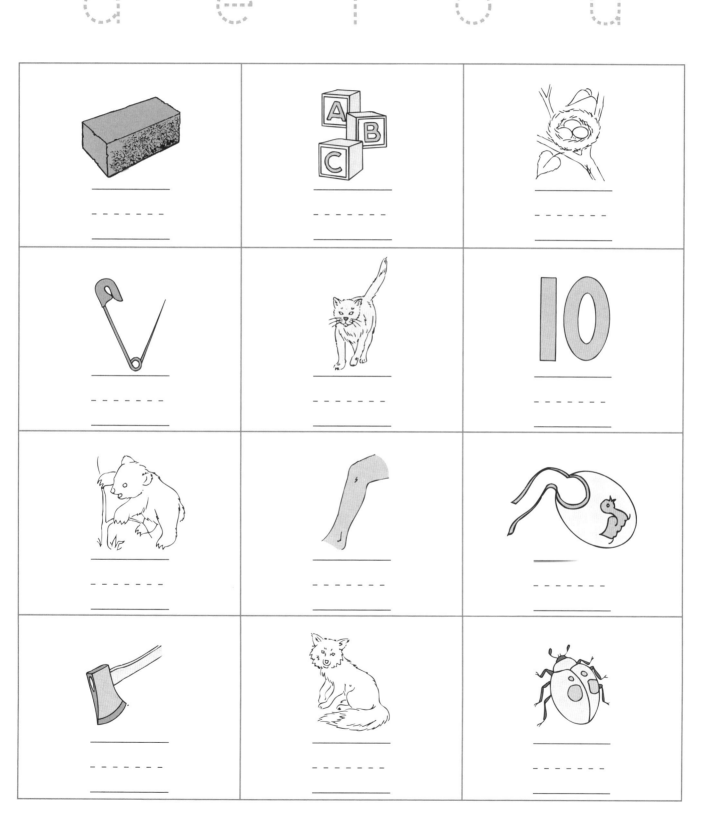

Review Short Vowels

Trace the letter and the mark of each long vowel sound. Write the vowel sound you hear in the picture name.

ā ē ī ō ū

Review Long Vowels

Write the letter or letters that stand for the long vowel sound you hear in the picture name. Put a line over the vowel.

ā ē ī ō ū

Write the letter that stands for the short vowel sound you hear in the picture name.

a e i o u

Review Short and Long Vowels   23

Trace the letters **ea** to finish each picture name.

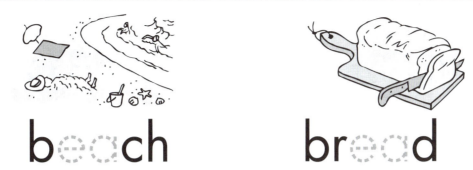

b__ea__ch   br__ea__d

Write the letters **ea** to finish each picture name. Say the word. If **ea** has the sound of ē as in **beach,** circle ē in the box. If **ea** has the sound of e as in **bread,** circle e in the box.

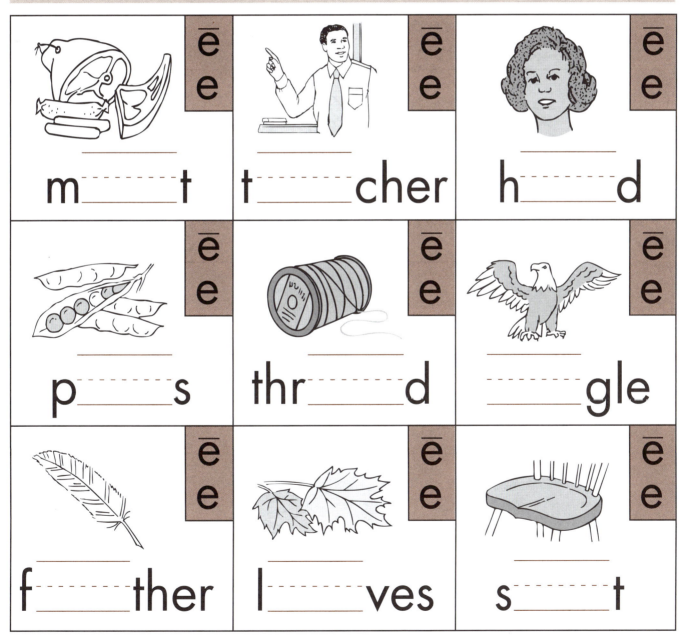

m____t   t____cher   h____d

p____s   thr____d   ____gle

f____ther   l____ves   s____t

Two Sounds of the Letters **ea** 25

Trace the vowel and **r** to finish each picture name.

perch   bird   purse

Trace the vowel and **r** at the beginning of each row.
Write the letters to complete the word that names each picture.

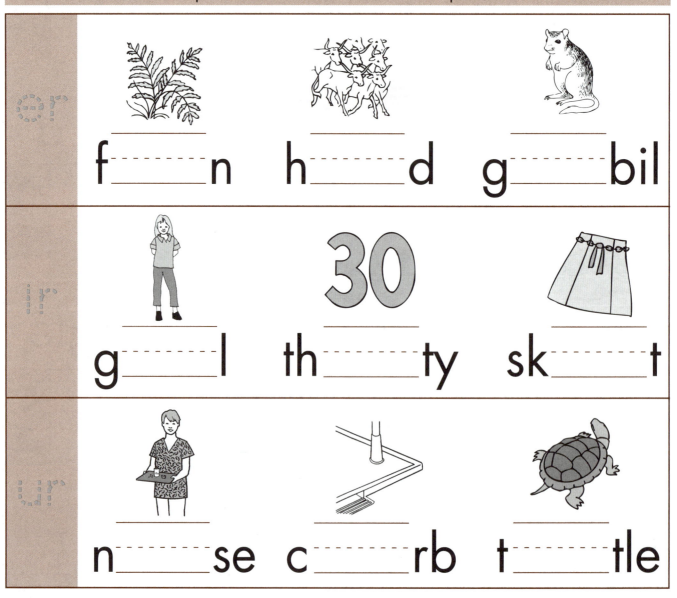

er
f___n   h___d   g___bil

ir
g___l   th___ty   sk___t

ur
n___se   c___rb   t___tle

26 Sounds of the Spellings **er**, **ir**, and **ur**

Trace the vowel and **r** in each picture name.

Write the two letters that complete the word that names the picture.

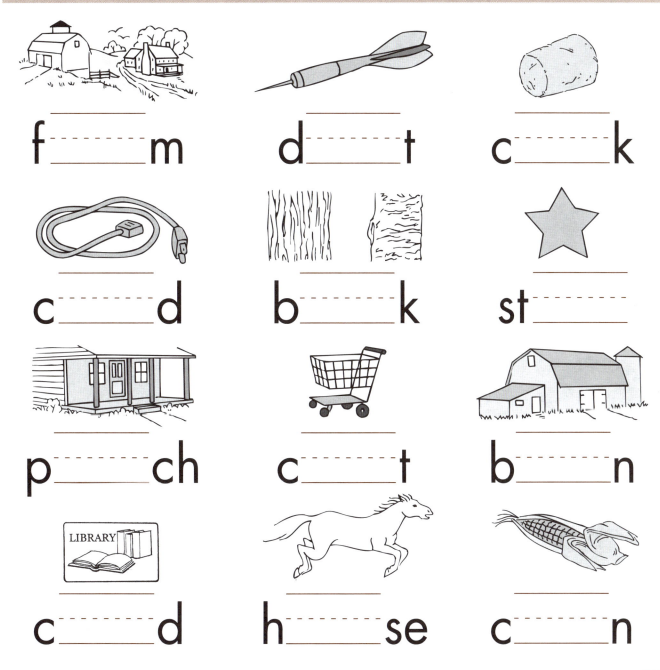

Sounds of the Spellings **ar** and **or**   27

Circle the letters that stand for the sound you hear in each picture name.

squirrel	or / ir / ar	cart	ir / er / ar	cord	er / or / ir
horn	ur / ar / or	circles	ir / ar / or	server	ar / ur / or
mouse	er / or / ar	arm	ar / ir / or	fern	or / ar / er
turtle	or / ur / ar	fork	ar / or / er	bird	or / ir / ar
garden	er / ur / ar	sink	or / ur / ir	cows	ar / er / or

28 Review Sounds of the Spellings **ir**, **er**, **ur**, **or**, and **ar**

Two letters together that make one sound are called a digraph.
Trace the digraph to finish each picture name.

 sheep   13 thirteen

Say the name for each picture. Write the letters to finish each picture name.

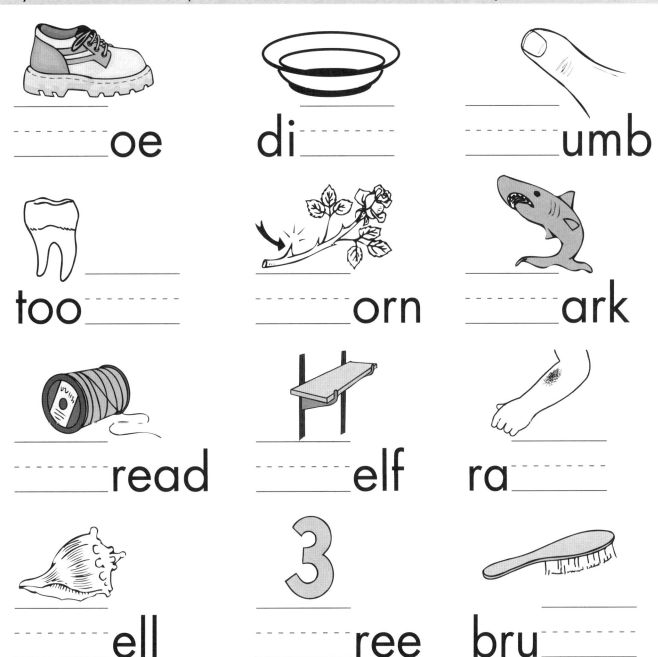

___oe   di___   ___umb

too___   ___orn   ___ark

___read   ___elf   ra___

___ell   ___ree   bru___

Consonant Digraphs **sh** and **th**   29

Two digraphs have the same sound.
Trace the digraphs to finish these words.

wa**tch**

cheek

pea**ch**

Say the name for each picture. Write the letters to finish each picture name.

in_____   _____air   ma_____

bea_____   _____ur   _____in

_____ick   pa_____   _____eese

30 Consonant Digraphs **ch** and **tch**

Trace the letters to write two more digraphs.

 ring

 lock

Write the name for each picture. The word will end with one of the digraphs.

ng | ck

Consonant Digraphs **ng** and **ck** 31

Trace the letters that stand for each digraph. Say the name for each picture. Write the letters that stand for the sound you hear at the end of the picture name.

sh ch th tch ck ng

32 Review Consonant Digraphs **sh, ch, th, tch, ck,** and **ng**

Trace the letter **c** to finish each picture name.

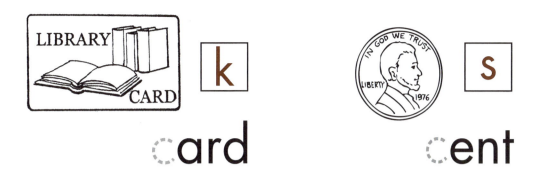

card   **c**ent

Write the letter **c** to finish each picure name. Say the word. If **c** has the sound of **k** as in **card,** write **k** in the box. If **c** has the sound of **s** as in **cent,** write **s** in the box.

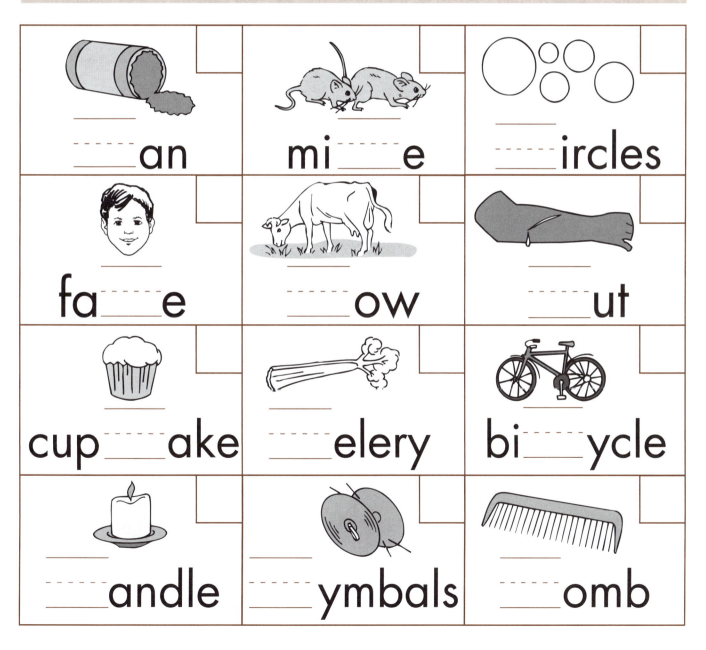

___an   mi___e   ___ircles

fa___e   ___ow   ___ut

cup___ake   ___elery   bi___ycle

___andle   ___ymbals   ___omb

Sounds of the Consonant **c** /k/ and /s/   33

Trace the letter g to finish each picture name.

g
goat

j
giraffe

Write the letter g to finish each picture name. Say the word. If g has the sound of g as in goat, write g in the box. If g has the sound of j as in giraffe, write j in the box.

ca__e	wa__on	__oose
fro__	pa__e	en__ine
__arden	__ym	bu__
oran__e	__erbil	__ame

34 Sounds of the Consonant g /g/ and /j/

Circle the letter that stands for the sound of **c** or **g** you hear in each picture name.

Review Consonants **c** and **g**

Consonant blends are two sounds that are often together.
Trace the consonant blend with **r** at the beginning of each picture name.

 brush

 frog

Say the name of each picture.
Write the consonant blend to finish each picture name.

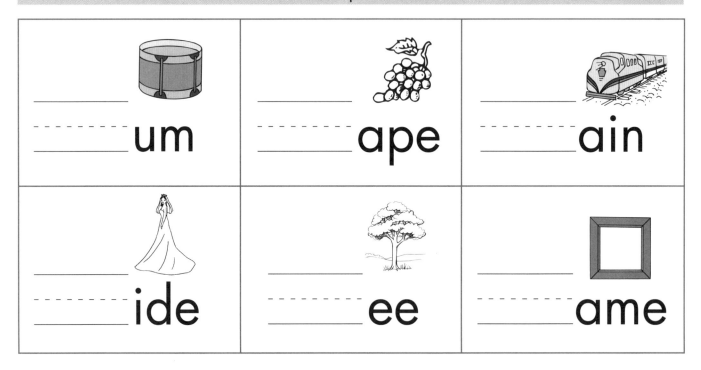

___um ___ape ___ain

___ide ___ee ___ame

Finish each sentence by writing one of the words below.

(grass   fruit   broom   print   truck   drink)

1. Apples and pears are _____.

2. Please _____ your name here.

3. Do not _____ the water.

36 Initial Consonant Blends with **r**

Trace the consonant blend with l at the beginning of each picture name.

 clock

 plate

Say the name of each picture.
Write the consonant blend to finish each picture name.

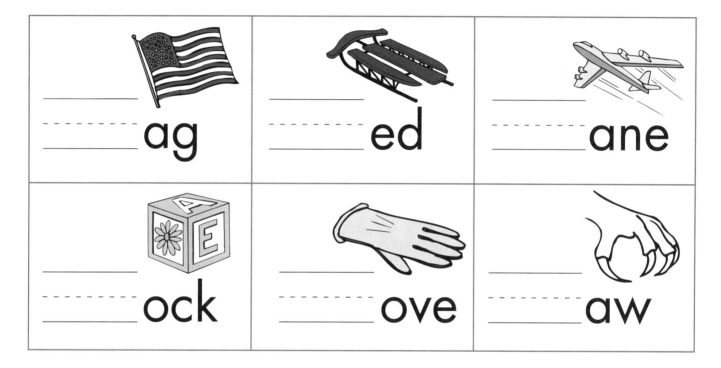

Finish each sentence by writing one of the words below.

(place   sleep   club   blue   glass   flower)

1. Pour the milk in the _____.

2. The baby has _____ eyes.

3. You can _____ in this bed.

Initial Consonant Blends with l **37**

Trace the consonant blend with **s** at the beginning of each picture name.

 snake    sled

Say the name of each picture.
Write the consonant blend to finish each picture name.

Finish each sentence by writing one of the words below.

smell   spin   step   snow   scare   skate

1. Snakes do not _____ me.

2. I can _____ the pizza.

3. You can sit on the top _____.

38   Initial Consonant Blends with **s**

Trace the **nd** in **hand**, the **nk** in **sink**, and the **nt** in **elephant**.

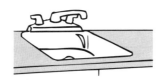

ha**nd**   si**nk**   elepha**nt**

Below each picture, write the missing **nd, nk,** or **nt**.

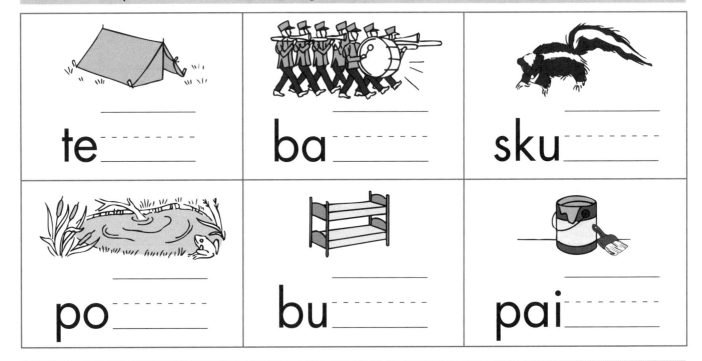

te____   ba____   sku____

po____   bu____   pai____

Finish each sentence by writing one of the words below.

pink   paint   behind   plant   trunk   found

1. Fran is walking _____ Lee.

2. This is a _____.

3. Put the box in the _____ of the car.

40   Final Consonant Blends with **n**

Trace the **lf** in **shelf**, the **ld** in **child**, and the **lt** in **colt**.

Below each picture, write the missing **lf, ld,** or **lt**.

go_____ be_____ ba_____

Finish each sentence by writing one of the words below.

wolf   cold   shelf   felt

1. That dog looks like a _____.

2. The rain _____ warm on my face.

3. It was too _____ to go outside.

4. The _____ is filled with books.

Final Consonant Blends with l

Circle the letters that stand for the sound you hear at the end of the picture name.

wolf	nd / **lf** / nk	belt	ld / **lt** / nt	thermometer	ld / nk / nt
hand	lf / lt / **nd**	elephant	**nt** / nd / lf	quilt	nd / nt / **lt**
shelf	ld / **lf** / lt	skunk	**nk** / nd / lt	—	lf / lt / ld
bunk	**nk** / lf / nt	pond	lt / **nd** / nt	tent	**nd** / nk / nt
golf	lt / **lf** / nd	trunk	**nk** / nt / ld	paint	**nt** / lt / nd

42   Review Final Consonant Blends

Trace the **wh** in **whistle** and the **mb** in **crumbs**.

whistle

crumbs

Write the missing **wh** or **mb** for each picture name.

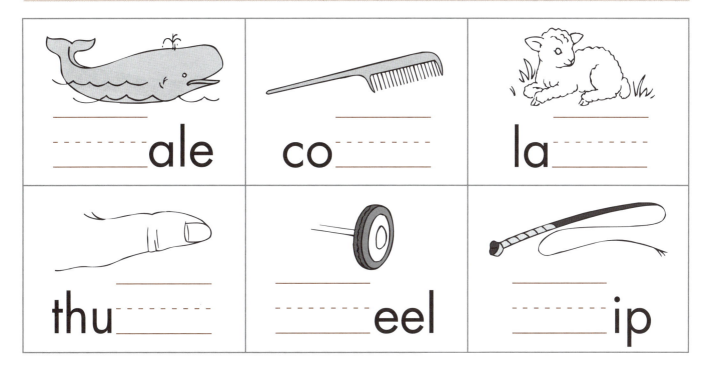

____ale   co____   la____

thu____   ____eel   ____ip

Finish each sentence by writing one of the words below.

thumb   white   comb   while   climb   when

1. Draw your picture on _____ paper.

2. Cats like to _____ trees.

3. Do you know _____ you are leaving?

The Spellings **wh** and **mb**

Trace the **kn** in **knob** and the **wr** in **wreath**.

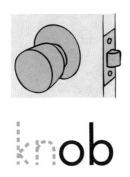
knob

wreath

Write the missing **kn** or **wr** for each picture name.

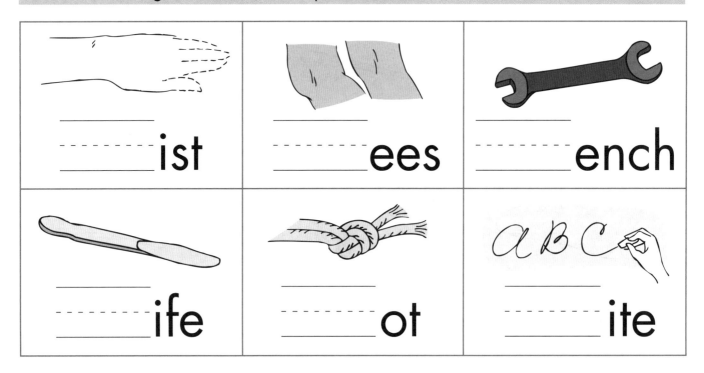

____ist   ____ees   ____ench

____ife   ____ot   ____ite

Finish each sentence by writing one of the words below.

wrong   knocked   knew   write   knees

1. Jill _____ the glass over.

2. That clock has the _____ time.

3. Please _____ your answer now.

44   The Spellings **kn** and **wr**

Write the missing letters to finish each picture name.

kn   wr   wh   mb

__ist (wh)	__ale (wh)	co__ (mb)
__eel (wh)	__ife (kn)	__ench (wr)
thu__ (mb)	__istle (wh)	__ob (kn)
__eath (wr)	__iskers (wh)	__ite (wr)
__ot (kn)	la__ (mb)	__ee (kn)

Review the Spellings **kn, wr, wh,** and **mb**   45

Trace the **oo** in each picture name. Say the words.

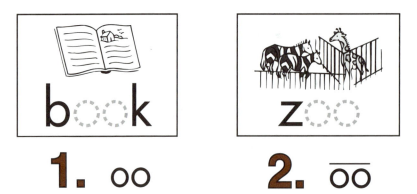

1. oo
2. o͞o

Write the missing **oo**. If the **oo** in the picture name has the **oo** sound in **book**, write 1 in the box. If it has the sound of **o͞o** in **zoo**, write 2 in the box.

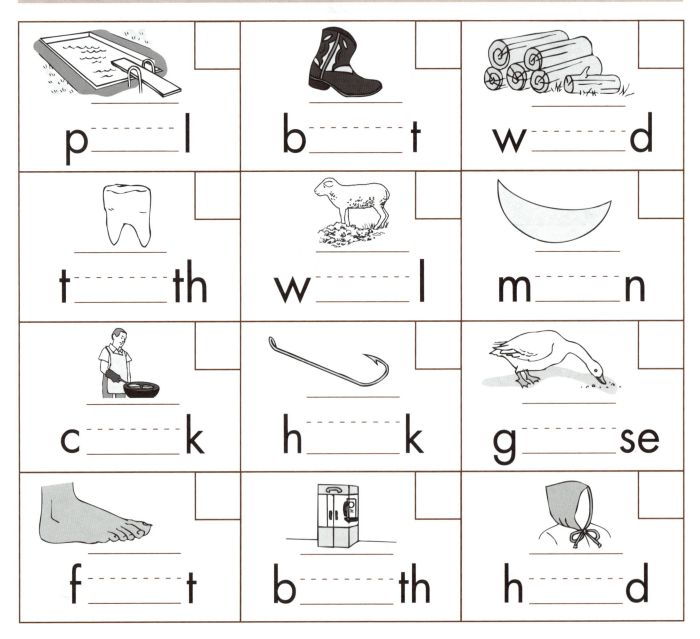

46 Sounds of the Spelling **oo**

Trace the **ou** or **ow** in each picture name. Say the words.

1. ou **2.** ō

Trace the **ou** or **ow** in the picture name. If the **ou** or **ow** has the sound of **ou** as in **clouds** or **ow** as in **cow,** write 1 in the small box. If it has the sound of **ō** as in **dough** or **snow,** write 2 in the small box.

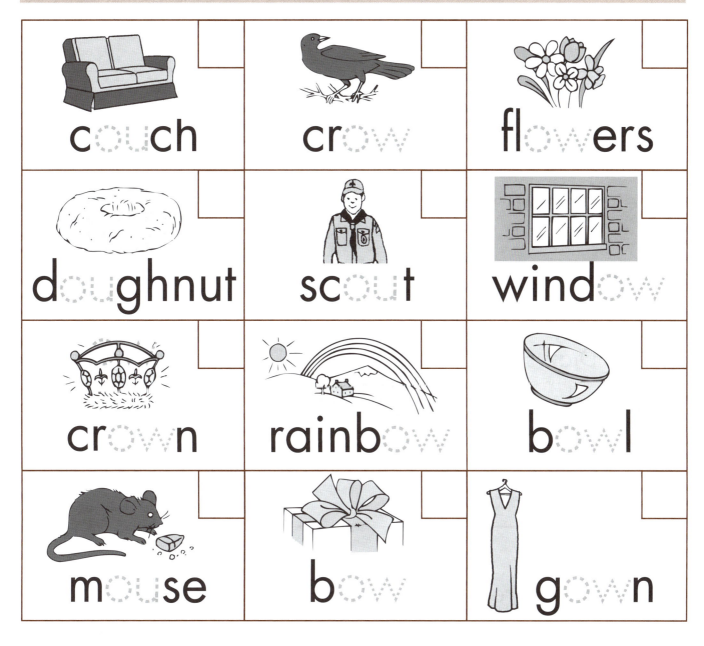

Sounds of the Spellings **ou** and **ow**

Trace the oi in coins and the oy in boy.

coins

boys

Finish each sentence by writing one of the words below.

| voice noise boys pointed oil coin joy toy |

1. Jet airplanes make _____.

2. The dog is playing with a new _____.

3. Mr. Díaz spoke in a loud _____.

4. Two girls and two _____ ran a race.

5. Cara _____ to the nest in the tree.

6. Dad put more _____ in the car.

48 The Diphthongs **oi** and **oy**

Trace the letters **ear** in each picture name.

1. ear   **2.** bear   **3.** earth

Read each sentence. In the box write the numeral that tells which picture at the top has the same sound of **ear** that you hear in the underlined word.

☐ Judy wants to <u>wear</u> her new shoes.

☐ Do you <u>hear</u> the dog barking?

☐ Eric went to bed <u>early</u>.

☐ Chris likes to eat <u>pears</u>.

☐ Walk <u>near</u> the side of the road.

☐ Kayla <u>learned</u> to ride her bike.

Three Sounds of the Spelling **ear**

Trace the ew in the picture name.

scr(ew) — o͞o

Finish each sentence by writing one of the words below.

| chew threw drew grew flew new blew stew |

1. The bird _____ from tree to tree.

2. My dog _____ to be very big.

3. Alex _____ up the biggest balloon.

4. Dogs like to _____ on bones.

5. Grace _____ a picture of her dog.

6. Mr. Shaw bought a _____ car.

Finish each sentence by writing one of the words below.

> ball   straw   crawled   tall   call   all
> paws   walk   sidewalk   walls   saw   talked

1. Jen and Sam ate _____ of the cake.

2. You need a _____ to drink this juice.

3. Do not ride your bike on the _____.

4. The cat is washing its face and _____.

5. This _____ building has ten floors.

6. The teacher _____ about rockets.

7. Please _____ me when dinner is ready.

8. We painted the living room _____.

9. The _____ rolled across the street.

Sound of the Letter **a** Before **ll, lk,** and **w**   51

Write the letters that stand for the vowel sounds you hear in each picture name.

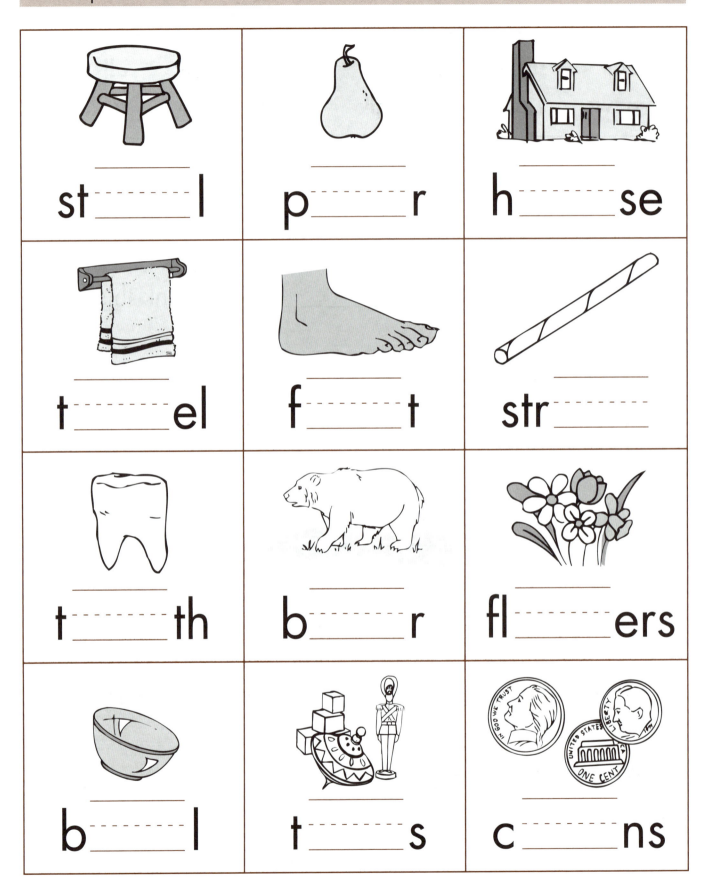

52 Review Vowel Digraphs

Trace the consonant and the ending that are added to each word.
Say the new word.
Add the correct consonant and ending to each word in the list.

sun + n + y	sit + t + ing	stop + p + ed
fun + __ + ____	get + __ + ____	rub + __ + ____
bag + __ + ____	hop + __ + ____	pet + __ + ____
star + __ + ____	put + __ + ____	step + __ + ____

Finish each sentence by adding the correct consonant and ending to one of the words below. Write the new word on the line.

> pet   star   fun   hop   bag   get   step   stop

1. A rabbit was _____ in the yard.

2. The children _____ the new cat.

3. My dad is _____ a haircut.

4. The clown has a _____ face.

Doubling the Final Consonant Before Adding -y, -ing, and -ed

Trace the **i** and the ending that have been added.
Say the new word. Write the new word by changing **y** to **i**
and adding the correct ending to each word in the list.

baby + i + es — babies	cry + i + ed — cried
hurry _____	dry _____
penny _____	fry _____
pony _____	carry _____

Finish each sentence by changing **y** to **i** and adding the correct
ending to one of the words below. Write the new word on the line.

> hurry   carry   baby   penny   pony   fry   dry   pretty

1. We can ride on the two _____.

2. I _____ the dishes after supper.

3. Jeremy _____ the heavy box.

4. The cook _____ two eggs.

5. Pat _____ across the street.

Each key word has been changed to form a new word.

sun + n + y — sunny	run + n + ing — running
dry + i + ed — dried	try + i + es — tries

Finish each sentence by changing the ending to one of the words below. Write the new word on the line.

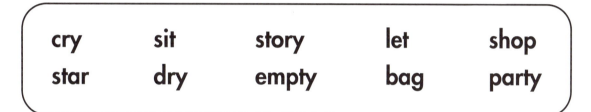

cry   sit   story   let   shop
star   dry   empty   bag   party

1. Ms. Walker reads many _____ to us.

2. We _____ for shoes yesterday.

3. Marco went to three _____ last week.

4. It was a bright, _____ night.

5. Who keeps _____ the cat go out?

6. Bob _____ the bottle into the sink.

7. Ellen is _____ on the front steps.

Changing Root Words Before Adding -y, -ing, -ed, or -es

The letters **s** and **es** are added to make a word mean more than one. Trace the **s** that is added to **pen** and the **es** that is added to **peach**.

pen   pens   peach   peaches

Below each picture circle the ending that stands for the sound you hear at the end of each picture name.

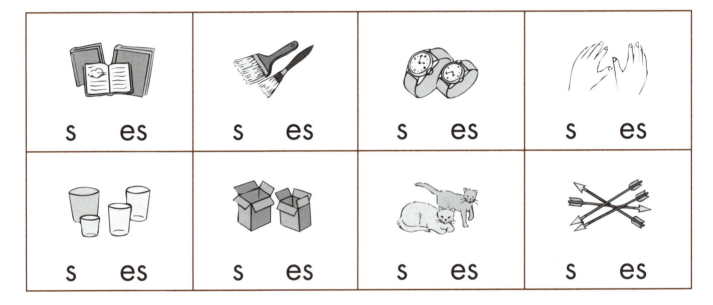

Finish each sentence by writing one of the words below.

branches   locks   foxes   nests   buses

1. We ride to school on _____.

2. There are two _____ on the door.

3. The _____ have no leaves.

56   Adding -s or -es to Form Plurals

If a word ends in **e**, you must drop the **e** before you add these endings.

bak~~e~~ + ed   piec~~e~~ + es   writ~~e~~ + ing   rac~~e~~ + r

baked   *pieces*   *writing*   *racer*

In these lists, cross out **e** at the end of each word. Add the ending and write the new word on the line.

-ed

like _____

name _____

save _____

hope _____

-es

bridge _____

house _____

bounce _____

prize _____

-ing

come _____

give _____

store _____

hide _____

-er

dance _____

joke _____

ride _____

skate _____

Each picture name is changed to make it mean more than one.
Trace the new words that mean more than one.

hat + s   glass + es   bab~~y~~ + i + es

hats   glasses   babies

Change these words to make them mean more than one.
Write each new word on the line.

wish _____   cherry _____   family _____

ranch _____   tail _____   ship _____

Change the words in each box to make them like
the key word. Write each new word on the line.

bag + g + y
baggy

fun _____
sun _____

pet + t + ing
petting

stop _____
plan _____

shop + p + ed
shopped

spot _____
trap _____

dr~~y~~ + i + ed
dried

carry _____
cry _____

Review Adding Endings

Change the words in each box to make them like the key word. Write each new word on the line.

sun + n + y
sunny

bag _____

star _____

run + n + ing
running

cut _____

win _____

hop + p + ed
hopped

plan _____

dot _____

carry + i + ed
carried

spy _____

worry _____

Change these words to make them mean more than one. Write each new word on the line.

picture + es
pictures

box + es
boxes

baby + i + es
babies

lunch _____   dish _____   fence _____

city _____   face _____   circus _____

watch _____   puppy _____   nose _____

Review Adding Endings **59**

Trace the ending **-ly** added to **quiet** and the new word **quietly**.
Add **-ly** to each word in the word list. Write each new word on the line.

quiet + ly — quietly

deep _____   soft _____

real _____   even _____

slow _____   close _____

warm _____   loud _____

Finish each sentence by using one of the words from above.

1. Cars moved _____ through the snow.

2. Matt dressed _____ to go ice skating.

3. I am _____ hungry and want to eat now.

4. Jasmine spoke so _____ that no one heard her.

5. Line up the books _____ on the shelf.

6. We are _____ related to each other.

7. The bell rang _____.

Trace the ending **-ful** added to **hope** and the new word **hopeful**.
Add **-ful** to each word in the word list. Write each new word on the line.

hope + ful — hopeful

thank _____   play _____

color _____   help _____

pain _____   cheer _____

tear _____   care _____

Finish each sentence by using one of the words from above.

1. Remember to be _____ on your bike.

2. A cut finger can be very _____.

3. We were _____ that the rain stopped before the picnic.

4. The _____ puppy chased the squirrel through the park.

5. Tom was very _____ at the book fair.

6. The _____ lady sang a song.

7. The leaves are _____ in fall.

The prefix **un-** means "not." Add **un-** to each word in the word list. Write each new word on the line.

fair   unfair

kind _____   happy _____

clear _____   wise _____

able _____   safe _____

real _____   even _____

Finish each sentence by using one of the words from above.

1. I felt _____ when my cat was lost.

2. The short girls are _____ to reach the tree branch.

3. The teams will be _____ if one has more players.

4. After the rain, the lake was _____ for ice skating.

5. Do not be _____ to the kitten.

6. The name on the paper was _____.

The prefix **re-** means "again." Add **re-** to each word in the word list. Write each new word on the line.

read   reread

pay _____   run _____

join _____   print _____

use _____   place _____

wind _____   cycle _____

Finish each sentence by using one of the words from above.

1. We can _____ the team next year.

2. You must _____ the newspapers.

3. Joel wants to _____ his letter.

4. Please _____ the lamp you moved.

5. Dad will _____ the kite's string.

6. Let's _____ the DVD and watch the movie again.

7. I will _____ you when I earn the money.

Add the ending **-ful** or **-ly** to the words in the first column.
Add the prefix **un-** or **re-** to the words in the second column.
Write the new word on the line.

-ful -ly	un- re-
use _____	tied _____
help _____	able _____
color _____	locked _____
quick _____	used _____
friend _____	play _____

Finish each sentence by using one of the words from above.

1. That tool is not _____ for this job.

2. We must walk _____ or we will miss the bus.

3. Your shoe is _____.

4. The _____ puppy wagged its tail.

5. The door was _____ so we went in.

6. We _____ the plastic bags.

Review **un-**, **re-**, **-ly**, and **-ful**

On the line, write the prefix or ending which has been added to each base word.

retie	_____	slowly	_____	replay	_____
safely	_____	unkind	_____	unclear	_____
careful	_____	tearful	_____	warmly	_____
unfair	_____	repay	_____	hopeful	_____
sadly	_____	wisely	_____	playful	_____
cheerful	_____	untrue	_____	rerun	_____

On the line, write the ending which has been added to each base word.

zoos	_____	cried	_____	dropped	_____
baked	_____	dishes	_____	starry	_____
bigger	_____	pans	_____	ponies	_____
hiding	_____	driver	_____	stepping	_____
bones	_____	funny	_____	hurried	_____
hopping	_____	cities	_____	boxes	_____

Review Prefixes and Endings

A compound word is made of two words. In each group, draw lines to connect two small words that can make a compound word. Say the new word. Then write the compound words on the lines.

flag	nut	_____
corn	crow	_____
pea	pole	_____
scare	field	_____
pan	walk	_____
side	shelf	_____
rain	cakes	_____
book	bow	_____
snow	house	_____
bird	tie	_____
door	way	_____
neck	balls	_____

Compound Words

A compound word is made of two words. Read the words in the list. Decide which words in the list are compound words. Draw a line between the two words in the compound words. Then write the compound words on the lines.

something	sideways	yellow	without
father	classroom	maybe	careful
everyone	birthday	popcorn	snowman
sailboat	parade	blueberry	cowboy
spaceship	airplane	children	seesaw
surprise	window	morning	after

Compound Words

A contraction is a short form of two words. The words are put together, and a letter or letters are taken out. An apostrophe (') is used in place of the letters. Trace the contractions in the list of words.

is not	isn't	are not	aren't	was not	wasn't
do not	don't	does not	doesn't	did not	didn't
can not	can't	has not	hasn't	have not	haven't

Finish each sentence by using one of the contractions above.

1. I _____ in school today.

2. Josh _____ finished drying the dishes.

3. Maria _____ like cheese.

4. We were late because we _____ leave until seven o'clock.

5. _____ sit on the wet steps!

6. You _____ got time to watch TV.

7. We _____ going on vacation this year.

8. Bridget and Olivia _____ come to the party.

Contractions with **not**

A contraction is a short form of two words. The words are put together, and a letter or letters are taken out. An apostrophe (') is used in place of the letters. Trace the contractions in the list of words.

| you have | you've | she is | she's | we are | we're |
| they will | they'll | he would | he'd | I am | I'm |

In each group, draw a line from the words to their contractions.

we are	he's	you are	they're
you have	we're	I would	he'll
he is	he'd	they are	I'd
she will	you've	they have	you're
he would	she'll	he will	they've

Finish each sentence by using one of the contractions above.

1. I think _____ got my gloves.

2. Mara says _____ ready to go home.

3. _____ help you if I could.

4. They said _____ come today.

5. Jack said that _____ be late.

6. I am glad _____ my best friend.

Contractions with Pronouns

Read the story. Look for five places where you can use a compound word. Write the compound words in the first list. Then look for five places where you can use a contraction. Write the contractions in the second list.

We have put up a flag pole in front of our house. It is near the drive way. Dad says he will put the flag up in the morning. At sun down, Mom will take it down. We are going to get a spot light, too. I know how to fold the flag, but I need some one to help me. I can not do it myself.

Compound Words

_____

_____

_____

_____

_____

Contractions

_____

_____

_____

_____

_____

Review Compound Words and Contractions

A syllable has one vowel sound. Many words have more than one syllable. Say the picture names aloud. Listen for the vowel sounds. Trace the number in the box.

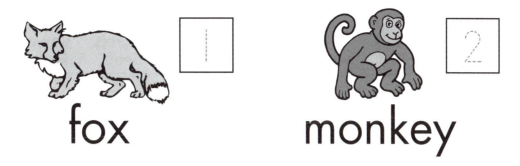

fox   monkey

In each box write the number of vowel sounds, or syllables, you hear in the picture name.

Syllables

On the first line, write the number of vowel letters you see in each word.
On the second line, write the number of vowel sounds you hear.
On the third line, write the number of syllables in each word.

	Vowels Seen	Vowels Heard	Syllables		Vowels Seen	Vowels Heard	Syllables
garage	___	___	___	believe	___	___	___
maps	___	___	___	might	___	___	___
remove	___	___	___	noise	___	___	___
asleep	___	___	___	farmer	___	___	___
unpack	___	___	___	break	___	___	___
unload	___	___	___	someone	___	___	___
school	___	___	___	people	___	___	___
rope	___	___	___	lion	___	___	___
pull	___	___	___	cookie	___	___	___
straight	___	___	___	calf	___	___	___
hello	___	___	___	leave	___	___	___
please	___	___	___	across	___	___	___
told	___	___	___	zoo	___	___	___
wagon	___	___	___	cellar	___	___	___
three	___	___	___	giant	___	___	___

Vowel Sounds and Syllables

Sometimes you need to divide a word with more than one syllable. If a word has a double consonant, divide between the two consonant letters. Trace the dividing line in the first picture name. Draw a line to divide each picture name into two syllables.

pup|py	mittens	dollar
	button	pillow
raccoon	cherries	kitten	carrots
balloon	puppet	butter	penny

Dividing Syllables—Double Consonants

Sometimes a word with two syllables has two different consonants between vowels. Then you can divide between the two consonants. Trace the dividing line in the first picture name. Draw a line to divide each picture name into two syllables.

basket

picnic

pencil

curtain

chimney

turkey

penguin

garbage

garden

chipmunk

helmet

lantern

sixteen

If a word ends in **le** and a consonant comes before **le**, divide before the consonant.
Trace the dividing line in the first picture name.
Draw a line to divide each picture name into two syllables.

Dividing Syllables—Consonant Before **le**

Draw a line to divide each word that has more than one syllable.

ball	leaf	winter	mirror
doctor	circus	once	April
certain	heard	cattle	ground
goat	catch	hunt	letter
twice	bottle	dinner	bounce
middle	game	friend	message

Write the above words in the correct list below.

One-Syllable Words

_____   _____   _____
_____   _____   _____
_____   _____   _____
_____   _____   _____

Two-Syllable Words

_____   _____   _____
_____   _____   _____
_____   _____   _____
_____   _____   _____

Review Syllables

Say each word. Circle the letter that stands for the vowel sound in the word.

hand	clock	leaf	fire	tube
a ā	o ō	e ē	i ī	u ū

milk	nest	bone	tub	cake
i ī	e ē	o ō	u ū	a ā

feet	duck	pipe	rain	fox
e ē	u ū	i ī	a ā	o ō

Write the word for each picture name.

_____

_____

_____

_____

_____

_____

Assessment 77

Say each picture name. Write the two letters that stand for the consonant blend you hear at the beginning of the word.

Say each picture name. Write the two letters that stand for the consonant digraph you hear at the beginning or end of each picture name.

Write the word for each picture name.

Say each picture name.
Write the word under the picture.

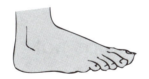

Assessment **79**

On the line after each word in this group, write the plural form of the word.

judge _____   watch _____

lady _____   piece _____

dolphin _____   bottle _____

nose _____   glass _____

street _____   fox _____

On the line next to each pair of words, write the contraction for the words.

1. you will _____   6. she is _____

2. does not _____   7. could not _____

3. let us _____   8. they are _____

4. I have _____   9. I am _____

5. are not _____   10. has not _____

Finish each sentence. Write the correct form of the word at the beginning.

baby 1. There are three _____ in the nursery.

cry 2. All of them are _____ now.

run 3. Two boys are _____ around.

chase 4. They are _____ each other.

lunch 5. Soon they will all have their _____.

Assessment **80**